CONTENTS

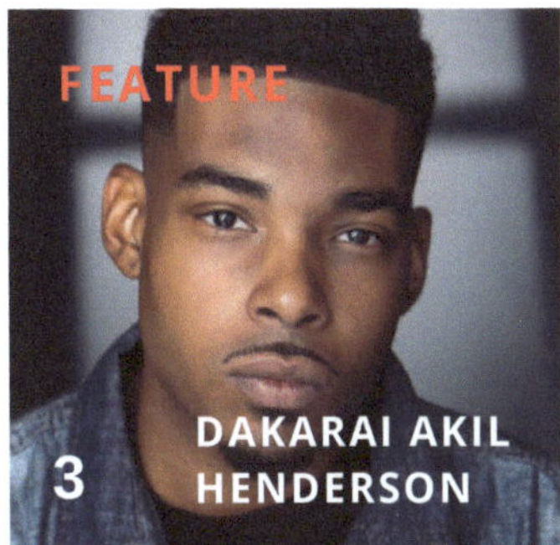

3 DAKARAI AKIL HENDERSON

8 ENTERTAINMENT ARTIST: TRINITI ALANA

FASHION: PAINSTITCH

DAKARAI
AKIL HENDERSON

Houston native, tenacious, imminent actor Dakarai Akil Henderson is an[3] all-around professional in the film industry. The talented star is not only an actor but also a Screenwriter, Director, and Producer.

The professional filmmaker has acted in over 15 prominent films, and 10 are now streaming on various platforms, including Apple TV, Amazon Prime, Tubi TV, VUDU, and Peacock. The star actor is known for the popular feature film, The Dirty 3rd: The Next Generation, where he starred alongside Clifton Powell, Chico Bean, and Propane.

This was one of his favorite and most memorable films. He waited over six hours for an audition just to be told that auditions were closed. But Dakarai was adamant about doing the audition, and as we all know today, he got the role.

DIRECTORIAL DEBUT

Dakarai Henderson enjoys acting because it allows him to bring other people's ideas and characters to life. But, this year, the actor made his directorial debut. He released his very own feature film, *The Hooper*. Henderson wrote and starred in the movie as well. He says that *The Hooper* is also one of his favorite movies because he got to see an idea in his mind become a reality as the film has over 100,000 views on Tubi TV.

The admirable Actor, Director, and Producer have five more film projects releasing this year as Dakarai looks forward to releasing the feature film *PIGS*. The film has already won the "Best Film A... in New Orleans, Louisiana. This one of the first movies Dakarai starred in. The producer flew him Atlanta, Georgia, for the role. Dakarai is eager for the release of *PIGS* because he was not supposed to act in it but instead memorized the script a week before filming.

"DON'T BE AFRAID TO BE DIFFERENT."
-DAKARAI AKIL HENDERSON

While speaking with Dakarai, he reminds us of the importance of motivation and hustle. He reveals as a kid, he'd never fit in but knew he served a bigger purpose. The filmmaker does what he loves and says, "Don't be afraid to be different."

The actor's ultimate goal is to be a household name like Idris Elba and Denzel Washington. He wants to star in prominent roles that make worldwide box office films, including Marvel and DC Universe.

By: Valencia Lee
Editor in Chief

Follow Dakarai Akil Henderson on Instagram @Dakaraiakil3d

4

THE
HOOPER

SUPER HUMANS HAVE MASTERY OVER THEIR EMOTIONS, WHO TAKE JOY IN SIMPLY EXISTING AND CREATING ABOVE ALL ELSE.

SUPER
HUMAN

TRINITI
ALANA

Born and raised in Houston, Texas, Triniti Alana found her love for music when she was only a toddler. At 17 years old, the singer and songwriter decided to pursue and dedicate all of her time to her music. The artist quit her job and stopped playing tennis, and in December 2022, the ambitious and goal-oriented artist released her first album, "Lovesone."

Triniti Alana's music is diverse, with various genres such as pop, hip-hop, chopped and screwed, and R&B. Some of her favorite artists include Syd, Miguel, and Beyoncé. She adds that one day she hopefully follows in the footsteps of these influencers.

The "Lovesone" artist has a unique vocal range and has been promoting and performing songs from her album, with the single "Sexy MF" at the peak. During Triniti Alanna's performances, you can tell her music means the world to her as she gives lots of energy and emotion. The audience has no choice but to vibe with her. The young and talented artist enjoys creating and writing music everyone can relate to, as her music is based on real-life experiences. One of her favorite things about being an artist is hearing her completed projects in the studio.

Triniti Alana's goal for 2023 is to travel while performing and promoting her new album, "Lonesome." The singer and songwriter plans to release a music video soon. But her overall goal is to learn to produce and engineer music and ultimately master the craft of being a prestigious female artist.

STREET
100
the
HEAT

Homestead Slim

LIVE
MONDAY &
WEDNESDAY
@ 7:00 PM

WWW.STREET100THEHEAT.COM

SHEBOU BOUTISH

START YOUR

BUSINESS

The most popular business brands SheBou carries are youngkwon100playz , Trensetta Trinkets and Go Ghetta Nation Apperal. Two of which are ran by Go Ghetta Nation Youngprenuers.

COMPANY GOALS

Company goals are to carry more brands, both established and start-up. Also to become a powerful asset for her surrounding communities.

Check Out Business Facebook Page
SHEBOU BOUTISH

5 N. 4th St
Beaumont, Texas
77702

SOCIAL MEDIA OUTLETS

theofficialcnoteslim
INSTAGRAM
Jacquelynsells
(nonanylevel)
INSTAGRAM

TERRY MONTGOMERY

Terry Montgomery is known for his high energy and ability to always bring a good time. You may have seen Terry at a club as he actively and aggressively promotes events and artists in Dallas, Texas, and East Texas. Terry puts all of his energy behind the artists and businesses he believes in. He is also a part of Top-Notch Entertainment.

By: Valencia Lee

Top Notch Entertainment

Top Notch Entertainment consists of Terry Montgomery, Keith Palmer, Teddy Rivers, Lee Palmer, and Denton. The guys grew up together and have known each other since the 8th grade. Although the guys are adults now and live in different cities and states, they host an annual BBQ in Irving, Texas, and thousands of people attend and celebrate.

Top Notch Entertainment celebrated their 16th annual *Nawf Side BBQ* this year. The event was held in mid July and there are events all weekend. They have free food, live performances, a deejay, games, vendors, networking, and an after-party. Last year, **Top Notch Entertainment** hosted their first BBQ in East Texas and plan to host another one this year on Labor Day.

MANAGING ROMANTIC RELATIONSHIPS WITH A PARTNER THAT HAS A MOOD DISORDER

Rhonda Williams
M.S. Counseling Psychology, LPC - A

LOVE IS IN THE AIR

When you meet that special someone and their pheromones are speaking directly to your pheromones, everything is total bliss. You finally found someone who speaks your love language, is attentive, faithful, and supportive; I'm talking about the crème de la crème of the relationship pool$_{13}$Finally, you can exhale... Until you meet that unwanted third party in your relationship that will always be there in some capacity. How do you sustain the love and passion that brought you together after that unwanted guest peeks its head in? After experiencing the goodness that the "highs" have to offer... Can you weather the storm when introduced to the "lows"?

WHAT IS A MOOD DISORDER?

A mood disorder is a mental health state that affects an individual's emotional sentiments. One can experience extended periods of extreme sadness and/or happiness with a mood disorder. Other adverse variables may be present depending on the condition, such as anger, impatience, and irritability. Mood disorders can affect an individual's ability to complete daily activities, and behavioral adjustments are undoubtedly present.

Bipolar and depression and their subtypes are the two commonly known mood disorders that are talked about; however, there are a couple more that are very real and can impact relationships negatively if gone unidentified and untreated: Premenstrual dysphoric disorder (PMDD) and Disruptive mood dysregulation disorder (DMDD)-(Impacts children and adolescents).

Mood disorders can affect anyone, no matter age, race, or gender. However, women are more susceptible to major depression than men; three common factors add to the progression of mood disorders: Environmental, biological, and genetic.

efore meeting the third party, the
omance was sweet, and the
nergy was high. When the mood
hanges, so do the feeling of love,
assion, security, and sexual desire
om both parties. When someone
experiencing an episode, they are
kely to experience irritability,
nger, and frustration, which
terferes with bonding, growth,
nd pleasure in a partnership. With
me the other party can share
eelings of neglect, insecurity,
nger, and dissatisfaction.
rofound changes and
npredictability of the patient's
ehavior often create volatility and
security in the relationship
zorin et al, 2021).

consistency, along with the lack
f security, is a combination of
eakening a relationship. Not only
an it impact relationships
entally and emotionally, but
nancially as well, depending on
nancial habits during episodes,
npulsive spending, gambling,
iling to pay bills, and not going to
ork due to mental state.
epending on the couple, such
abits can affect the household
emendously and add more
ressors and obligations to the
artner. Not to mention individuals
ho self-medicate and fall into an
ddiction to street drugs or those
ho participate in at-risk sexual
ehavior. So many aspects to
onsider.

It is the responsibility of the
individual diagnosed to ensure that
they are in their best mental state
to be a good partner.
Understandably, some people do
not like how prescribed psych
medication makes them feel or the
negative connotation associated
with taking drugs, causing some to
abstain from using them as
prescribed. Therefore, those who
suffer from a mood disorder must
understand what the condition
entails and how it affects them
personally. What are your triggers?
What do your highs and lows look
like? What behaviors do you
display? Are you taking your
medications as prescribed? Should
you speak with your care provider
to adjust the care plan if
warranted? These are the
necessities that one must consider
to maintain a sense of self-
awareness and understanding. Yes,
self-awareness is essential, but
maintaining a healthy lifestyle that
benefits your mental state will
make a difference in what's
manifested in life.

It is the partner's responsibility to be honest with themselves if having a person with a mood disorder is something they are willing to take on. No matter how it's viewed, individuals have the right to decide if they want to take on the responsibility of committing to a relationship with someone who is bipolar or manically depressed. It's ok to walk away early before causing more hurt or damage to a person or the relationship. It is perfectly fine to dissolve a relationship that does not serve you for the greater good If the person is not doing what they need to maintain a healthy well-being.

For example, suppose they are not taking their meds, practicing healthy coping skills, abstaining from reckless behavior, and not showing up in the relationship as they should. In that case, it is not much you can do because what they are dealing with is internal. No one should take abuse, no matter the reasoning. Understanding boundaries and if your presence is beneficial or enabling to the partnership is critical.

If one decides to build a future with an individual with a mood disorder, some things can be done to preserve the love and passion for each other, especially during intense episodes.

1. **Separate the person from the effects of the disability.**
2. **Continue to support your partner in seeking/maintaining professional help.**
3. **Continual research on the disorder.**
4. **Practice self-care and create a safe place to retreat in stressful times.**
5. **Do the work.**
6. **Plan ahead**
7. **Create a secure word/phrase (timeout) when things get too intense.**
8. **Couples Counseling**

Love with an individual with a mood disorder can still be magical if both parties create it with one another. Remember what attracted you to one another and how it felt to fall for each other. Create new memories, fall in with each other daily, and love without conditions.

Reference

Azurin, J. M., Lefrere, A., & Belzeaux, R. (2021). The Impact of Bipolar Disorder on Couple Functioning: Implications for Care and Treatment. A Systematic Review. Medicina (Kaunas, Lithuania), 57(8), 771. https://doi.org/10.3390/medicina57080771

SPREAD LOVE EVERYWHERE YOU GO. LET NO ONE EVER COME TO YOU WITHOUT LEAVING HAPPIER!
-MOTHER TERESA!

Pain Stitch~4k13

" I DO WHAT I
DO WITH A
PASSION ...
WITH ALL THE
PAIN I HAVE! "
Katrina, Owner

Contact at:
Instagram: Painstitch4k13
Facebook: Painstitch4k1

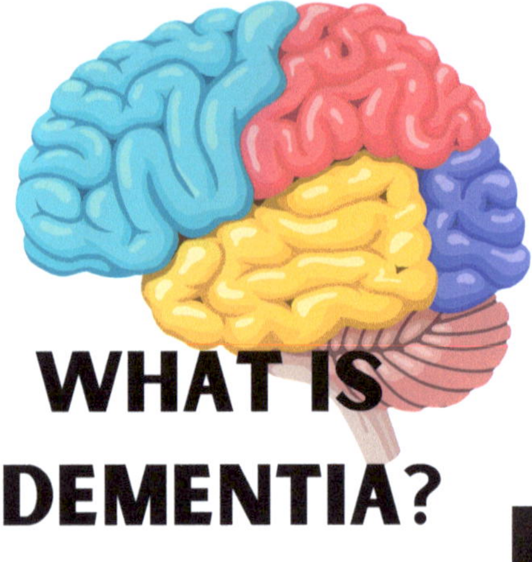

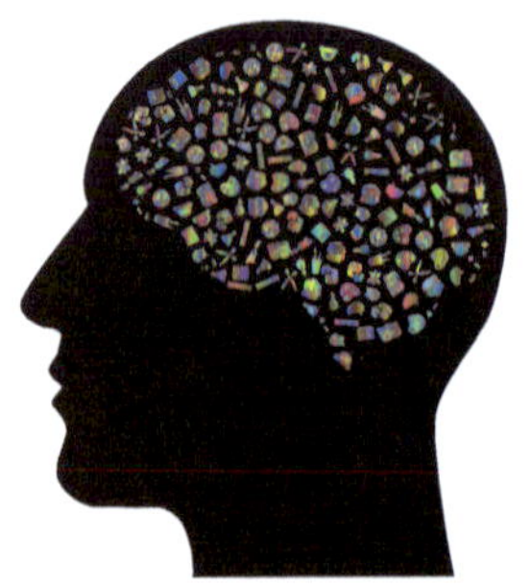

WHAT IS DEMENTIA?

Dementia is not a specific disease but covers a wide range of specific medical conditions caused by abnormal brain changes. The symptoms include memory loss, limited social skills, and impaired thinking abilities. The incurable disorder typically affects people over 65, but there have been cases reported of people in their early 30s affected also.

Altztymers disease is the most common cause of dementia, but there are many other disorders and conditions linked to dementia also. These disorders affect not only those experiencing symptoms but also those around them. Most people who suffer in the later stages of dementia cannot care for themselves independently and need help.

One can lower the risk factors for dementia by a change in diet and exercise, stopping excessive alcohol and smoking, diabetes, depression, and vitamin deficiency. You can also keep an active mind, such as writing, reading, and solving puzzles. Unfortunately, there are still many things doctors are unaware of with dementia, but with self-care, we can lower the chances of us getting dementia and affecting our family and relationships.

Valencia Lee
EDITOR IN CHEIF

Lost Your Mind

Written by: Valencia Lee/ Illustrated By Asia Penelton

YOU WERE A NURTURER, OUR GLUE, AND ALWAYS
HELD EVERYTHING TOGETHER. EVERY DIFFICULT
MOMENT AND HEARTBREAK, YOU ALWAYS MADE
MY LIFE BETTER.
EVEN THE SIMPLEST THINGS, IT WAS YOU WHO
ALWAYS KNEW WHAT TO SAY TO ME.
BUT NOW I HAVE LOST MY IDENTITY BECAUSE
YOU LOST YOUR MEMORY.
WE USED TO TALK ABOUT EVERYTHING, NOW I
DON'T EVEN GET A REPLY.
WE PRAYED WITHOUT CEASING, BUT WE HAD TO
RETURN YOU TO THE BIG GUY.
THINKING BACK, YOU TOLD ME REPEATEDLY THAT
YOU WERE LOSING YOUR MIND, BUT I DIDN'T
BELIEVE IT.
NOW I WATCH YOU LAY HOPELESSLY, AND
TOGETHER, WE GRIEVE.
MY EXPECTATIONS WERE FOR YOU ALWAYS TO BE
HERE.
THE LAST THING YOU SAID TO ME WAS I LOVE
YOU, AND I DROWNED MYSELF IN TEARS.
WHEN YOU LOST YOUR MIND, I LOST A PIECE OF
MY HEART.
IRREPLACEABLE, YOU WERE THE ONE WHO LOVED
ME UNCONDITIONALLY FROM THE START.
THERE IS NEVER A DAY THAT GOES BY THAT I
DON'T THINK OF YOU.
WHEN LOVE FINDS ME, I HOPE IT'S SOMEONE WITH
THE SAME CHARACTERISTICS AND VALUES.

In Loving Memory of Jeneline Turner

DR. ROBIN TURNER

The multi-talented entrepreneur, former Army Veteran, and former CEO, Dr. Robin Turner, holds many titles and responsibilities. She always leads by example, and walks by faith.

One of the most inspiring features about Dr. Turner is she feels the greatest gift of all is love. As she runs multiple pharmacies, she has raised 12 children and four of her own. As she was naturally born with the gift of giving and always putting others first, the former Army veteran was diagnosed with breast and ovarian cancer in 2008. Dr. Turner's faith was tested and she was forced to put herself first. But today "The Survivor" testifies that she is cancer-free and stressed-free

The accomplished and resilient leader is always in good spirits and keeps busy operating her pharmacies, serving others, and raising and loving children.

Dr. Robin Turner was recognized as a Woman Entrepreneur in Texas by one of our time's greatest and most influential voices, Dr. Maya Angelou.

Dr. Robin Turner continues to take the world by storm as she operates multiple businesses. She is also an author, singer, and songwriter. The entrepreneur manages her daughter Triniti Alana, Del Muzic, and JtheSinger's music careers.

Dr. Robin Turner desires to use her talent and past experiences to inspire and motivate others to be their best every day because tomorrow is not promised.

CHAIN REACTION: UNLEASHING THE POWER OF BLOCKCHAINS

By: Robert Bazile, Jacob Tadesse, & Micheal Duvall

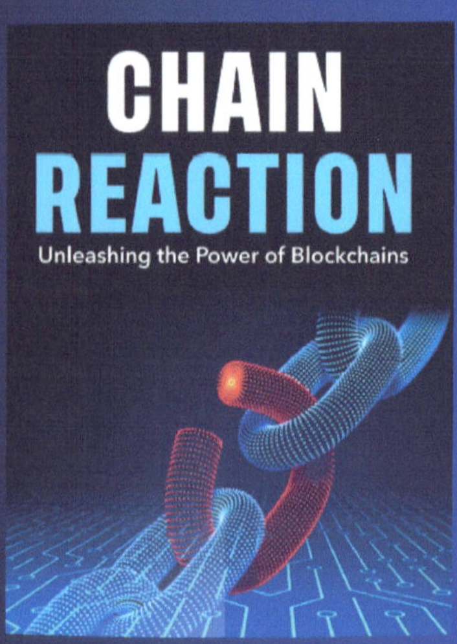

AUGUST 2023

The Beautiful PROBLEM

Wisps of smoke rise against a deep purple and orange sunrise. Cold water splashes against the young man's face. He stretches and then sets off down the red-ochre path he has walked daily, undeterred by the distance for the last three years. This isn't any ordinary man. He is a visionary.

Growing up in eastern Uganda during the 1990s and 2000s could, on any given day, be a young boy's dream. Ichode Erasmus would guide his herd of cows through the tall grass and swamps of the bush, play bows and arrows with his friends, and fall asleep to the gentle whooshing of his cows' tails, his belly full of fresh mango, laying in the shade of acacia trees.

But in the dead of night, he would return to the same bush, this time hiding, with his elderly grandmother, desperate for shelter from armed insurgents. Tesoland was at the grips of a decades-long insurgency fueled by a lack of government protection. The raiders would target villages under the cover of darkness. Ichode and his community grew hesitant to dream about better days as there was no certainty when life might return to normal. And so, for a decade of his life, he danced a delicate balance between this bucolic life of a cattle herder by day and the threat of death by moonlight. At 15, Ichode had seen more death than a soldier on the front lines. The bodies he saw, lifeless, stacked along the roadside, were not those of a foreign enemy but of his village mates and relatives.

"Don't be surprised when this school is a leading University of Africa one day. A University for all those who can't afford school but who also can't afford to be quiet." -Ichode Erasmus, Founder

When others sought escape from their nightmares, something within Ichode pulled him away from the drinking joints. His drive was relentless, propelling him toward experiences others discouraged him from. He knew, he could feel it in his bones, that he was here for a purpose above his own desires. And so, set-back after set-back, he followed his insatiable drive to do something different from the status quo.

After completing University in Cyber Security, he traveled out of Uganda to west Africa on missionary work. Still, this wasn't his calling. He felt that same pull, urging him to return home to his community. His once thriving village was now slowly building back, barely surviving. Buildings still lay in ruins. Homesteads remained abandoned. The cattle herds never regained their numbers. It was a place of deep sadness, but Ichode could not keep himself away. And so he began picking his neighbors up and encouraging them to have hope in the future. Exasperated people laughed in his face, and continued living in response to the trauma that consumed their dreams. Make no mistake, this decline was not their own fault. This was the legacy of colonialism, still plaguing people in the 21st Century. What could they do, but focus on getting food for the day? They didn't have the energy to dream of better.

It did not phase Ichode, and in time he had gathered a small group of community members who recognized that together, they could plant the seeds of resiliency and positiv change. A community organization was born. The first thing they did was to identify orphaned children and ensure someone woul deliver food to them regularly. It wasn't food purchased. It was the little off-the-top each member could bear to give up. The number of kids they delivered to grew, and so did the helpers. They named themselves "Helping Hands Uganda."

The community kept hearing whispers of a young man rebuilding people's homes with n money! Who was he? "A witch doctor? Illuminati? That little man over there? No way!" But it was! Ichode's ability to nourish the memories of the community, and the way life was before the war, stirred inspiration in those around him. Little by little, more people joined him in his efforts. Soon, he was organizing free medical camps that served hundreds of people. Word spread fast, and with each new medical camp, people traveled further and further to receive medical care.

Somewhere along the way, Ichode found love and married a woman who also marched to the beat of her own drum, whose passion for service mixed seamlessly with his. Amelia Mayer was one of those few people who also felt the same force propelling her toward community activism. Amelia and Ichode collided, and a new galaxy of possibilities was born. Together, they launched a village ambulance service and organized their communities to sponsor life-changing medica procedures for people from villages who thought the rest of the world had forgotten them.

Erasmus & Amelia Icode, Founders

After years of working together to bring medical services directly to the area through strategic partnerships, and loyal donors, Ichode and his wife Amelia accepted that the real challenge was breaking the cycle of poverty and healing the generational trauma that was crippling their community. And so, the Ethan Ellsworth Vocational Skills Training Center was born. The two of them worked in the US, Amelia's home country, for a year and a half, saving up enough funds to build a school independently. Family, friends, and strangers donated funds for sewing machines, tools, and furniture.

The training center doors opened for its first classes 12 days before COVID-19 took the world by storm. Only two months after opening, the center was shuttered, along with all learning institutions, in what would become the world's longest school closure.

By February 2020, clouds of locusts descended upon the region from the Arabian Peninsula. As the last hatchlings decimated all greenery in sight, a drought rolled in, followed by flooding. Crops failed, and along with them, the hope of families who enrolled their children in Ethan Ellsworth's training programs. Fears of the end of the world ravaged what Ichode fought so tirelessly for.

Finally, in October 2020, the President announced that all schools could begin classes again. Before Ichode could dress himself the following morning, people were slamming their hands on the metal door to his room. "Wake up! We've come for registration!" "My daughter needs to graduate. She only has one month left to finish training!" "Ichode, we are waiting for you, oh!"

Erasmus rushed to the school to find old students and new faces lined under the porch, shielded from the sun in the intense morning light. Then, after months of vanquishment, students were ready to resume their learning, and they had brought friends and neighbors along, too!

That first class of students graduated from their respective courses, and land job placements with various partnerships Ichode and Amelia secured over the years of their community work.

Within only two years, the student population was bursting at the seams. The local council informed Ichode that he must make arrangements to move into a larger facility. It was a beautiful problem to have!

In the strange but rewarding way that this world and life work, a very generous donor caught wind of "The Beautiful Problem" and donated the down payment for a new plot of land. Now, the only thing stopping Ichode's dream is the funds for a new structure. His hope is for communities worldwide to be inspired by his and his community's story of resilience and persistence in the face of severe adversity and to come together to build this new school.

The Ethan Ellsworth Vocational Skills Training Center is located in Kolir, Bukedea District, Uganda, closer to the border of Kenya than the Ugandan Capitol. You can visit their website at www.livingtogetherinlove.org .

100% of donations go toward making this dream possible.

SUPER HUMAN
CLOTHING
COMING SOON!

SUPERHUMANS
HAVE MASTERY
OVER THEIR
EMOTIONS AND
TAKE JOY IN
SIMPLY EXISTING
AND CREATING
ABOVE ALL ELSE.

Have Joy in
Existing &
Creating

courage

Tameka Denise was born & raised in Dallas, Texas, the kingdom business mogul is a minister, life insurance broker, mentor, author, business coach, and speaker who remains dedicated, faithful, and committed to her calling..

THATSTAMEKADENISE.COM

JUST LASH IT

Just Lash It, Founder Felecia Johnson, will celebrate fou
years of business this year in September. It all started
when her family moved from the small town of Clovis,
New Mexico, to the big city of Dallas, Texas. Johnson wa
determined to establish independence. So the bold
entrepreneur created a business where she empowered a
women to be beautiful and confident in who they are.

Just Lash It carries
eyelashes and
lipstick for women
of all races. Johnson
doesn't just sell
these products but
provides an
experience to her
customers that they
will not get
anywhere else.

By: Valencia Lee

The bold, courageous business owner provides free consultations to her customers. For instance, if you are a beginner, Johnson has a process to determine what works best for you. She finds out what you like, gives you different options, and shows you how to apply your eyelashes and lipstick. She also has an excellent fashion sense and can tell you what to rock with your self-assured look.

Felecia Johnson confidently believes in what she does as she always rocks her bold, eccentric lipstick colors and hosts classes on mixing lipsticks and applying eyelashes.

The audacious stylist is passionate about her customers and the example of how women can be purposeful, appealing, and independent all in one. *Just Lash It* products are high quality. Some women who have purchased eyelashes from Felecia have lasted longer than three years. Their lashes are still in good shape. Another skill Johnson has is showing how to care for the products you purchase from her.

Felecia started her *Just Lash It* with only six pairs of eyelashes and has grown tremendously. Her goal in the future is to empower and help other women start their own businesses. She would also like to visit homeless women, battered women shelters, and cancer treatment centers to beautify them with her products and make them feel better and more confident about themselves.

BE
YOUR
OWN
#1
FAN
SUPER
HUMAN

THE YOUNG KING

history there are true stories about a
ung king who was really fond with the
nple things, such as clothes and family.
t after finding out the miserable
ings behind those beauty the world
splayed he learned something much
ore valuable. He learned about other
ople's miseries that made him wiser.
the end of the story, he was crowned
the greatest power of God Himself. He
ll learns the games of society and how
e world displays things to influence his
tion, so still kingkwon100playz !!
termined to gain the benefits of
editation that not only Russell
mmons discussed, but Oprah Winfrey,
be Bryant, Lebron James, and many
hers practiced. I've studied successful
ople my entire life, and this is the one
mmonality they all have.

iginally, Meditation was a thing for
nks and Buddists, but it has been
entifically proven that meditation has
any benefits, and I recommend
eryone practice it.

King Kwon's story has a very
meaningful moral message,
especially for the young readers. So
he decided to create his own things
around him so he wouldn't end of
following the wrong guidance but
lead. As far as he was concerned, the
examples for example the music
industry was implying were
incorrect, but what did he know, he
was only 13. The world is difficult to
be understood by children, but
when a child experiences adversity
he quickly begins to understand.

KingKwon100playz

Continue following his YouTube
Channel Kingkwon100playz and find
out! As many young kings before him
his legacy has yet to be told! Thank you
for your support!

BENEFITS OF *Meditation*

By: Valencia Lee

Years after failing over and over again, I learned that I have control over nothing but only my thoughts. Your thoughts create your reality, so I knew I needed to change them. Although I didn't know how I began reading and researching, one of the first books I came across was Russell Simmons's *Success Through Stillness*. This book discussed the importance of controlling your thoughts and how mastering the ability to completely stop brings peace of mind, wealth, and success ultimately.

I'd never heard of anything like this but was willing to try it. It sounded simple enough. But learning to stop my thoughts was one of the most challenging things I've ever tried to master. When I woke up in the morning, the first thing I would attempt to do was stop my thoughts, but it felt almost impossible.

After battling mental health illness most of my life. I'd experienced anxiety and panic disorders, bipolar disorder, manic depression, and even attempted suicide. Mastering the craft of meditation was initially inevitable for me.

WHAT IS MEDITATION?

Meditation is the practice of mindfulness in which one stops their thoughts and focus on a particular object or specific thought, such as bible verses or positive affirmations. Meditation aims to empty the mind of negative thoughts and appreciate peace in the moment. There are various types of meditation.

Determined to gain the benefits of meditation that not only Russell Simmons discussed, but Oprah Winfrey, Kobe Bryant, Lebron James, and many others practiced. I've studied successful people my entire life, and this is the one commonality they all have.

Originally, Meditation was a thing for Monks and Buddists, but it has been scientifically proven that meditation has many benefits, and I recommend everyone practice it.

Types Of
MEDITATION

1. Mindful Meditation - Originated from Buddhist teachings and is the most popular form of meditation in the Western world. Great for beginners, as you observe your thoughts without judgment or emotion. This technique combines concentration and awareness.
2. Spiritual Meditation - This method is used in all regions and focuses on developing a deeper understanding of the spiritual realm and connecting to the source. For example, reciting bible verses and prayer.
3. Focused Meditation - includes moon gazing, body scan, staring at the flame of a fire, and concentrating on your breathing.
4. Movement Meditation - Good for people who find peace in action and make you present in the moment, including walking, gardening, jogging, and working out.
5. Mantra Meditation - prominent in Hindu and Buddhism traditions. This kind of meditation consists of using repetitive sounds to clear the mind. The most common word or phrase is "OM."
6. Transcendental Meditation - allows you to experience the depths of meditation. Best used when taught by an expert and includes mantras.
7. Visualization Meditation - Imagine yourself in a peaceful and positive environment accomplishing a goal. This type of meditation increases motivation and promotes inner peace.

Forced to master the art of meditation by any means necessary. At first, I was sick and nauseous. My body jerked uncontrollably. I realized that the feelings I was experiencing were all of the toxins and negative energy leaving my body. So I continued to stick with it. I tried to meditate all day. Finally, saying, The Lord's Prayer would calm my body. Before I knew it, I could go a minute, stopping my thoughts. Then it increased to 5 minutes. Then ten minutes. Now I can meditate for hours at a time.

WHY MEDITATE?

Our lives are full of noise, and we often find ourselves on the go. We seldom find time for silence and stopping the noise. In Psalm 46:10, GOD says, "Be Still and know that I am GOD." Everything GOD does is in silence. The trees and grass grow in silence. The Sun, moon, and stars rotate around the universe in silence. Music would be static if there were no silence between each note. Therefore, if we do not find time to meditate and clear our minds of the noise in our lives, then it will become chaos.

Initially, meditation will be difficult because you will be forced to face your struggles, flaws, and everything you do not find acceptable about yourself. But the end result will be freedom.

Benefits of MEDITATION

1. Self Aware
2. Reduce Anxiety
3. Increased Patience
4. Ability to manage stress
5. Focus on the present moment
6. Sleep Better
7. Reduce Pain
8. Boost Self Confidence
9. Reduces Inflammation
10. Improves Brain Health
11. Increase Self Control
12. Decreases Blood Pressure

I have been meditating for over four years now, and the benefits have been spectacular. I have become more self-aware and purposeful in my actions, reduced negative emotions, and increased patience and tolerance. Increase focus and increased productivity. Meditation allows you to let everything go and become present in the moment. It sounds simple, but the discipline to remain still for long periods can be very challenging at first, especially when you've never tried to do it before.

I meditate every morning. One of the first things I do is as if my body is downloading information from the Spiritual Realm, and I am receiving guidance for the day. It is impossible know God without experiencing silence.